Dropping In On...
ITALY

David C. King

A Geography Series

ROURKE BOOK COMPANY, INC.
VERO BEACH, FLORIDA 32964

A Blackbirch Graphics book.
Series Editor: Tanya Lee Stone

Printed in the United States of America.

Library of Congress Cataloging-in-Publication Data

King, David C.
    Italy / David C. King
        p.   cm. — (Dropping in on)
    Includes bibliographic references and index.
    ISBN 1-55916-084-5
    1. Italy—Description and travel—Juvenile literature. I. Title. II. Series.
    DG430.2.K56   1995
    914.504'929—dc20   94-37228
                                          CIP
                                          AC

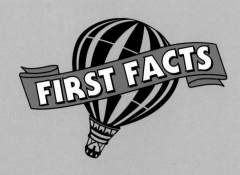

Italy

■ ■ ■ ■ ■ ■ ■ ■ ■ ■ ■ ■

Official Name: Italian Republic

Area: 116,500 square miles

Population: 57,800,000

Capital: Rome

Largest City: Rome

Highest Elevation:

Mount Rosa (15,203 feet)

Official Language: Italian

Major Religion: Roman Catholic

Money: Lira

Form of Government:

Democratic Republic

Flag:

TABLE OF CONTENTS

Our Blue Ball—The Earth

The Earth can be divided into two hemispheres. The word hemisphere means "half a ball"—in this case, the ball is the Earth.

The equator is an imaginary line that runs around the middle of the Earth. It separates the Northern Hemisphere from the Southern Hemisphere. North America— where Canada, the United States, and Mexico are located—is in the Northern Hemisphere.

The Northern Hemisphere

When the North Pole is tilted toward the sun, the sun's most powerful rays strike the northern half of the Earth and less sunshine hits the Southern Hemisphere. That is when people in the Northern Hemisphere enjoy summer. When

the North Pole is tilted away from the sun, and the Southern Hemisphere receives the most sunshine, the seasons reverse. Then winter comes to the Northern Hemisphere. Seasons in the Northern Hemisphere and the Southern Hemisphere are always opposite.

Get Ready for Italy

Hop into your hot-air balloon. Let's take a trip!
You are about to drop in on a small country that is
about the same size as the state of Arizona. Italy is
located on a peninsula—an area of land that is
surrounded by water on 3 sides. On the map, you
can see that the peninsula is shaped like a boot. The
toe of the boot almost touches the Italian island of
Sicily. Sardinia is another large island that is part
of Italy. More than 57 million people live on the
peninsula and the islands.

Italy is a warm, sunny country. Three sides of
Italy are bordered by 5 seas. In the north, there
are mountains called the Alps that separate Italy
from the rest of Europe.

Stop 1: Milan

The beautiful Galleria is a popular place to shop in Milan.

Our first stop is the city of Milan in the north of Italy. Milan is the second largest city in Italy.

At first glance, the city looks new, with its modern buildings. But Milan is more than 3,000 years old. Let's stop at a huge cathedral called the Duomo. The Duomo is one of the biggest churches in the world. Nearby is the Galleria, a large, glass-domed building. The Galleria is famous for its restaurants and shops. A block away is an opera theater called La Scala. Italy is famous for opera, and La Scala is called the greatest opera house in the world.

The countryside around Milan is one of the most beautiful regions in Italy. Farms are set among sparkling lakes and rivers, with the Alps towering in the distance. The hillsides are covered with vineyards, which provide grapes for Italy's wine industry. Wine, rice, wheat, and other products are shipped south to Genoa—Italy's largest seaport. Genoa is also known as the birthplace of Christopher Columbus, the great explorer.

The Duomo cathedral is decorated with more than 2,000 statues.

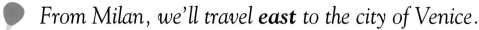 From Milan, we'll travel **east** to the city of Venice.

Here you can see a water bus, or vaporetti, *travel along Canaletto Way.*
Inset: While in Venice, let a gondolier *take you for a ride.*

Venice

Ligurian Sea

Adriatic Sea

Tyrrhenian Sea

Ionian Sea

Mediterranean Sea

N
W E
S

Stop 2: Venice

Imagine a city where all the streets are canals and people travel by boat instead of automobiles. That's what Venice is like. Venice is called "The City of Canals." More than 200 canals wind through the city and there are 400 bridges.

One way to travel around Venice is in a small boat called a *gondola*, steered by a boatman, or *gondolier*. Most people travel by big water buses known as *vaporetti*.

Venice was built as a seaport more than 500 years ago. There are many beautiful churches. The most famous church is the Basilica San Marco.

In Italy, there are hundreds of different kinds of pasta to eat.

The Foods of Italy

When you sit down to a meal anywhere in Italy, you are sure to eat well. The main meal will almost always include either rice or pasta. Spaghetti is one kind of pasta, but there are more than 200 other kinds. The pasta will be followed by meat or fish and vegetables, then a salad, fruit, and cheese. If you still have room for dessert, you might try a layered pastry or a cake.

One of the most important parts of Italian cooking is the freshness of the food. People like to go to the market every day to choose fresh food.

Each region of Italy has its own special dishes. In a northern restaurant, you might have a creamy rice dish called *risotto*, served with fresh fish and zucchini blossoms. In the central region, you can try thin noodles called *tagliolini*, with shrimp or lobster sauce. And in the south, a favorite dish is pasta cooked with octopus and asparagus, but you might prefer *zuppa de pesce*—fish stew.

Italian people can go to a variety of specialty markets to buy food. Here, a man shops in an outdoor fruit market.

*For our next stop, we'll head **southwest** to the city of Florence.*

Stop 3: Florence

Florence is located in the hilly central region of Italy, on the banks of the Arno River. Some parts of the city and its suburbs are very modern, but the central part of the city looks much as it did 500 years ago. In the 1400s, Florence became known throughout the world for its outstanding artists. And today, the city's museums hold some of the greatest paintings and statues in the world. Thousands of visitors come to Florence every year to view these works of art.

The city of Florence is filled with artwork. This beautiful mosaic decorates a ceiling.

From the Boboli Gardens you can see the whole city of Florence.

Florence has many beautiful, old churches and palaces. One of the most famous buildings is the Pitti Palace, which is now an art museum. Behind the palace are the Boboli Gardens, one of the most wonderful gardens in Italy. As you walk through the gardens, you pass many fountains and statues.

The city is also famous for its handcrafts. Florentine craft workers make wonderful items of lace, silk, leather, and precious metals.

A few miles from Florence is the town of Pisa. Pisa is best known for its famous Leaning Tower.

Now we'll travel **southeast** to the city of Rome.

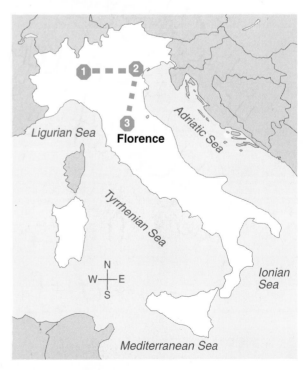

Stop 4: Rome

Rome is Italy's capital and its largest city, with nearly 4 million people. On the outskirts of the city, there are modern apartment buildings, offices, and stores. But in the central part of Rome, you will see mostly old buildings and ancient ruins. One of the ruins is the Circus Maximus.

The ruins of the Colosseum. In ancient Rome, 45,000 people could watch gladiators fight here.

In ancient Rome, 300,000 people would fill the Circus Maximus to watch chariot races. The most famous ancient building is the Colosseum, where fans watched gladiators fight.

Rome is always very crowded, noisy, and busy. The city has wide avenues, or boulevards. But there are also narrow, winding streets where many of the buildings are more than 400 years old.

The Spanish Steps are often packed with people.

If you follow one of the narrow streets, you will come to a place called the Spanish Steps. These wide, curved steps are a favorite gathering place. Nearby is one of the largest fountains in Rome, called the Trevi Fountain. People say that if you throw a coin into the fountain, you are sure to return to Rome.

In the center of Rome is a separate city called Vatican City. This is the home of the pope, the head of the world's Roman Catholic religion. Tourists come to Vatican City every day to visit St. Peter's Basilica, the largest church in the world. Next to the Basilica is the Sistine Chapel. Five hundred years ago, an artist named

St. Peter's Basilica was built in the 4th century, and is the most important Roman Catholic church.

Michelangelo painted scenes from the Bible on the ceiling of the Sistine Chapel. The paintings cover 10,000 square feet and took Michelangelo 4 years to complete.

Growing Up in Italy

Italian children can go either to public school or to one of the church private schools. From age 6 to 11, they attend elementary school. Children study the Italian language and grammar, math, history, science, and music. Most then go on to secondary school from age 11 to 14.

In Italy, there are many religious holidays, such as Christmas, Easter, Corpus Christi, and the Feast of the Assumption. At Christmastime, children receive their presents during the Feast of the Three Kings, instead of on Christmas day. The presents come, not from Santa Claus, but from a fairy-witch who is named Befana. The New Year is celebrated with noise and fireworks. The ancient belief was that the loud noise would frighten away the devil.

Italian schoolchildren on a field trip pose for a picture.

🎈 *Next, we'll travel **southeast** to Mount Vesuvius.*

Stop 5: Mount Vesuvius

As our balloon soars southeast along the coast, we pass over the busy city of Naples. The Tyrrhenian Sea curves into the land here forming the Bay of Naples. Small islands dot the sparkling blue waters of the bay. Many people flock here in summer to enjoy the beaches.

Mount Vesuvius's last powerful explosion was over 50 years ago.

On the southern edge of the bay, a mountain looms high above the coast. This is Mount Vesuvius, one of the most famous volcanoes in the world. Mount Vesuvius is quiet now. Its last big eruption was in 1944. The most amazing eruption took place almost 2,000 years ago. The ancient city of Pompeii and two towns were completely buried by volcanic ash and mud. Today, you can visit the ruins of Pompeii and the two towns.

Now, let's head **south** to the island of Sicily.

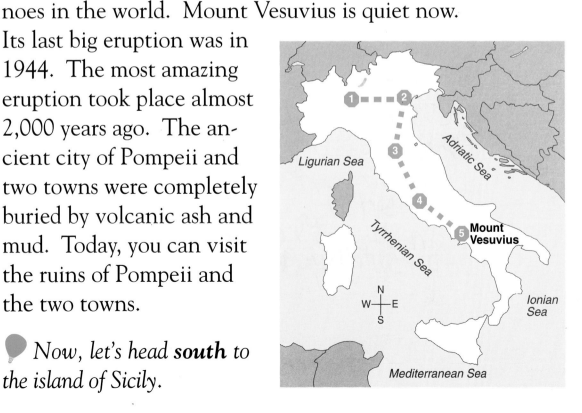

Stop 6: Sicily

The island of Sicily lies only 10 miles from the mainland of Italy. Sicily is about the size of the state of New Hampshire. It is the largest island in the Mediterranean Sea.

The beautiful town of Taormina sits at the edge of the sea.

The climate here is warm and sunny. Much of the island is mountainous. Most people live on the coastal plains, or level areas. The sunshine and warm temperatures make Sicily a perfect place for growing lemons and oranges. Island farmers also grow wheat, olives, and grapes.

One of the most popular towns is Taormina, on the east coast. If you look southwest, you see the huge volcano of Mount Etna. Another volcano, Mount Stromboli, is just off the north coast.

Life in a Farming Village

Farm families in Sicily and southern Italy have to work very hard. The soil is rocky and hilly. Because of this, farmers usually use sure-footed donkeys instead of farm tractors. The hot, dry climate also makes farming difficult. Irrigation channels are used to bring water to the fields from nearby rivers.

In the foot of Italy's boot, and on the offshore islands, farm villages are scattered through the hills and mountains. Some of the houses are made of stone with cone-shaped roofs. Others, called cavern houses, are carved directly into the hillside.

Both men and women work in the fields from dawn to dusk. They grow olives, vegetables, and grapes. On market days, the village streets are filled with colorful stalls. The villagers sell hand-made lace, wood carvings, baskets, and brightly colored clay whistles and pottery. A favorite pastime in the evening is a walk through the streets of the village.

For our final stop, we'll travel **northwest** *to the island of Sardinia.*

These white-washed cavern houses are cool inside even on the hottest days.

Stop 7: Sardinia

A Sardinian woman, in traditional dress, weaves a blanket on a loom.

Sardinia is the second-largest island in the Mediterranean Sea. It stretches 160 miles from north to south. Like Sicily, this is a sun-baked land of rugged mountains and hills. Small farm villages cling to the sides and tops of hills. Shepherds tend large flocks of sheep and goats. Goat cheese made in Sardinia is highly prized on the mainland.

The island also has wild ponies and donkeys. On Sardinia you can see the world's only white donkeys. Another breed of donkey grows no larger than a dog.

Thousands of people come from mainland Italy every summer for the beautiful white-sand beaches. In the hills above these beaches, you can explore the ruins of ancient stone fortresses. There are also large caves, called grottoes, carved out of the rock many centuries ago. Some of the grottoes are called "witches' houses." Others are known as "giants' tombs." While you explore the caves, you can make up stories about where these names might have come from.

At Costa Paradiso, people sunbathe near a clear, green-water lagoon.

Now it's time to set sail for home. When you return, you can think back on your wonderful adventure in Italy.

Glossary

bay An arm of an ocean or lake that cuts into the land.

gondola A small, narrow boat used on the canals of Venice.

grotto A cave or cavern.

irrigation A system for bringing water to farm fields through canals or channels.

island An area of land completely surrounded by water.

peninsula An area of land surrounded by water on 3 sides.

piazza The Italian word for a public square.

plain A flat or level area of land.

volcano A mountain that can erupt, sending up molten lava from deep below the Earth's crust.

Further Reading

Binney, Don. *Inside Italy*. New York: Franklin Watts, 1988.

Bisel, Sara. *Secrets of Vesuvius: Exploring the Mysteries of an Ancient Buried City*. New York: Scholastic, 1993.

Butler, Daphne. *Italy*. Madison, NJ: Raintree Steck-Vaughn, 1992.

Caselli, Giovanni. *The Everyday Life of a Florentine Merchant*. New York: P. Bedrick Books, 1991.

Clark, Colin. *Journey Through Italy*. Mahwah, NJ: Troll, 1994.

Hubley, John and Penny. *A Family in Italy*. Minneapolis, MN: Lerner, 1987.

Jarvis, Mary B. *The Leaning Tower of Pisa*. Mankato, MN: Capstone Press, 1991.

McClean, Virginia. *Pastatively Italy*. Memphis, TN: Redbird, 1994.

Index

Acknowledgments and Photo Credits
Cover: B. Wickley/SuperStock, Inc.; pp. 4, 6–7: National Aeronautics and Space Administration; p. 10: Ameller/Explorer/Photo Researchers, Inc.; pp. 11, 23, 28: Italian Government Tourist Board; pp. 12–13: ©Sylvain Grandadam/Photo Researchers, Inc.; p. 12 (inset): ©Will and Deni McIntyre/Photo Researchers, Inc.; p. 14: ©Richard Laird/Leo de Wys, Inc.; pp. 15, 22: ©W. Hille/Leo de Wys, Inc.; p. 16: ©Margot Granitsas/Photo Researchers, Inc.; pp. 17, 27: ©Giulio Veggi/Photo Researchers, Inc.; pp. 18–19: ©Steve Vidler/Leo de Wys, Inc.; p. 20: ©Catherine Ursillo/Photo Researchers, Inc.; p. 21: ©Susan McCartney/Photo Researchers, Inc.; pp. 24–25: ©Jeanetta Baker/Leo de Wys, Inc.; p. 29: ©Marka/Leo de Wys, Inc.
Maps by Blackbirch Graphics, Inc.